The Estate Agent's Daughter

Rhian Edwards

Seren is the book imprint of
Poetry Wales Press Ltd.
57 Nolton Street, Bridgend, Wales, CF31 3AE
www.serenbooks.com
facebook.com/SerenBooks
twitter@SerenBooks

ISBN: 978-1-78172-583-2
ebook: 978-1-78172-584-9

A CIP record for this title is available from the British Library.

The publisher acknowledges the financial assistance of the Books Council of Wales.

Cover photograph: Gareth L. Edwards Estate Agents, 4-6 Dunraven Place,
Bridgend, circa 1972.

Author photograph: Abeer Ameer

Printed in Bembo by Severn, Gloucester.

The Estate Agent's Daughter

For Megan

Contents

PART ONE

The Estate Agent's Daughter	9
Counting Boards	11
Fool's Errand	12
All the Terrors	13
Banjo Jims	14
The Larsen Trap (Four for a Boy)	15
House Share	17
Fourth Floor	18
Jocale (Five for Silver)	19
White Gold (Six for Gold)	20
Junk Metal	21
The Virtual Family (Eight for a Wish)	22
Something Else (Ten for a Bird That's Best To Miss)	23
This Was the Spring	25
Net Curtain	26
Argos Wedding	27
The Birds of Rhiannon	29
Blodeuwedd	30

PART TWO

It Is	35
Poems in the Dock	36
This Is The Drawer	37
"Describe The Pain"	38
The Abacus of Stamina	39
The Art of Fastening	40
Dear Rain	41
Threnody	42
David	44
Kay	46
Gareth	47
Free, No Obligation Valuation	48
Adam	49
I Remember Being You,	50
I Am Turning	51
Identity Theft	53

The Trees Have Dimmed   54
Return of the Native   55
Prodigal Audience   56

PART THREE

Thinner   63
He Is The Kind   64
My Clocks Pester Him   65
In A Relationship (Pending)   66
Circling   67
Slapstick   68
I Took The First Lust   69
Fatter   70
Love and Taxes   71
Handover   72
No Harm In Him   73
The Addiction Counsellor   75

Acknowledgements   76

PART ONE

The Estate Agent's Daughter

is sold as seen,
semi-detached,
in walking distance of Pen-
y-Bont ar Ogwr with all its mod cons,
located in a quiet hammerhead.

She has wrought iron gates,
hard standing parking for two.
Her pea gravel driveway sweeps
to a *Cloudy Apple* composite door,
stained window with leaded detail.

Her hallway is carpeted with sycamore
seeds and cherry blossom throughout.
Her white dogleg staircase leads to a spindle
gallery landing, with access to a loft
conversion with a skylight window.

Ground floor comprises open plan lounge/diner,
recesses either side of fire breast wall.
Her writing desk has been nudged to the brink
of the bay. Curtains may be drawn
around her to quarantine at will.

Dining table moonlights as tributary desk,
cable-knit cardigans draped across Ikea
chairs come as standard.
Spider-warding conkers mob
her laminated corners in vain.

She boasts a galley kitchen
with splashback tiling. Integrated
fridge/freezer, sunken spotlighting,
eye level oven (rarely used)
white goods to remain.

The master bedroom is in need of updating,
juliet balcony in state of disrepair.
Outside: She has a storm porch
with power and lighting,
chipped area to the side.

The estate agent's daughter retains
many original features, coved
ceilings, double glazing throughout.
Unsuitable for first time buyers,
no ongoing chain.

Counting Boards

Instead of I-spy in your Cortina,
we counted your *For Sale* boards:
The petrified, wooden flags of you,
the Austrian red, white stripes of you,
earmarked the houses for market.
as if the town was your game of *Monopoly.*

The black capitals of your name
fill the lines to the brim.
Your middle initial crowbarred in
to distinguish you
from the famouser you.

You taught me ratios by five-bar gating
the boards of your competitors:
Payton, Jewell & Caines, Porters,
Peter Alan, Peter Morgan, Reed Evans,
Bobby Powell of *Powell and Jones,*
the Sergeant Major who apprenticed you all.

I learned street names by solicitors,
hand-delivering fee notes, memoranda,
withdrawal, sale fallen through letters
to *Prossers, David & Snape, Whittinghams,*
R.L.Edwards & Partners, the legacy of Uncle Ronny,
who loathed his lawful life, the very practice
I was being groomed for.

After the abacus of board game, we drove
to your take-ons in silence. I dragged
the ribbon of the tape measure
to the corner of each room,
where you doubted my precision.
You confided more words to your dictaphone
than I could receive in a single tax year.

Fool's Errand

I've been strolling the aisles of *Tesco's* again,
bouncing the caged basket on my hip
like a lover ruminating in the park.

I have been learning the price gunners'
names by heart, abbreviating where I deem
necessary. I know the featured album of the week
verbatim. Watch me mouth each Adele lyric
without owning a note.

I have taken it upon myself to train
the fledgling shelf stackers. I send them
on scavenger hunts for perishables
that exist solely in my mind.

The peppered rocket cushions
the rattling of glass against metal,
as a bottle of £5 wine
seesaws the basket.

I catch glimpses of myself in the mirror
of the vegetable section. Look at me
fondling squash, inhaling beef tomatoes,
turning apples in my hand, like I have
any idea what on earth I am searching for.

All the Terrors

are gathered in this portmanteau,
this Hammmer House, this Ealing-made.
The razor cut of Cushing's cheeks,
hollowed eyes, RP that belongs to the Raj.

How I long for Christopher Lee, his oil-slicked
widow's peak, badger grey, immaculate cravat.
I would give the earth, mortality,
to be the trussed brunette in Regency.

Could my generous décolletage invite the screeches
of a fishing-lined bat to my Juliet balcony?
Or could the punctured cloud of my négligée
summon an unseasonable wind to my French doors?

Behold the jagged cloak, crimson lining, arms raised.
Regard as I back away in mugging fear,
mesmerised by the bloodshot white of his eyes,
all a swoon to the preachery of his pearly fangs.

Banjo Jims

Did I contrive the whole thing?
Banjo Jims on the corner of 700 East
and Ninth? Did I confetti sawdust
on the planks, strew the shavings
like morning grain for hens?

Was I the one who ivied the fairy lights
around the baroque mirror? Slopped bordello
red on the walls, dragged the salvaged
pew to the back of the stage. The Polaroid
montage at the bar, was that my own doing?

When I spun on the high stool
in my signature Charleston frock,
drinking bubbles in the afternoon;
was I the one who axed the ice
and remembered you first?

Was it me who tore the duct tape,
made a crude cross for your standing mark?
When I asked to borrow your guitar strap,
did I reverse angle the lens, close in
on your John Cusack features trying not to watch.

Did my vocal training pay off when I Merchant
Ivoried my accent, morphed into the familiar
foreigner for you? Was it you who tortured
the cliché and offered to buy the first drink?
Perhaps I fed you the line.

The Larsen Trap (Four for a Boy)

Magpies can be caught legally in Larsen traps,
a live-capture trap that uses a decoy bird to
lure others into the cage.

As foreign as a man could be:
Skin pale as a magpie's shoulder,
black feathered hair, a skullcap
of curls arranged in a chicanery
of tenderness.

A hooked Roman nose, aquiline,
Latin for eagle-like,
the certitude of a curved beak
that darted straight
for the stage.

He sang Country with a spurious
Texan twang, alien birdsong.
He plucked his own strings harshly,
souring the music, discording
the smallness of his voice.

I had him pegged as a Midnight Cowboy
freshly dismounted from the Greyhound,
what with his plaid shirt, weathered jeans,
a belt buckle that made him
a man of two halves.

He lived sparse as a monk in that uptown apartment,
shampooed his hair with a bar of soap,
boiled his coffee in a saucepan.
He capsized wooden crates for a desk,
a defeated dog on the couch.

I found his coarseness winsome.
Blurred by outlandishness, I mistook
his monosyllables for shyness,
his unkindness for grief,
his incursion for love.

The metronomic pecking, the incidental
score of us, came from a savage remoteness.
A coldness that scaffolded
a birdcage inside the hollow
of the hooded nest.

House Share

Your lethargic Labrador has nothing to impart.
She has licked every inch of this small apartment,
brailled it with her tongue, re-read it a thousand
times. This apartment is a dog-eared novel,
laced in saliva. She raises a solitary
eyebrow at my entrance, pricks up
her envelope flap of an ear.
She trots to my side as we stare
into the chasm of the fridge,
abandon all hope. I slump on the settee,
she circles her cushion, collapses
into a coil of herself.

How long have we been sleeping? She laps
at her paw, her crotch, my wrist,
drifts back into her coma. Even my stabs
at conversation bore her. She only comes
to life for that hour when we chance
the outside. I spellbind her
with a tennis ball, unravelling the silk
of her spit as she drops it at my feet.
I swear she is as grateful as I am
to return to this box room apartment,
the jaundiced settee, the *Coke* crate desk,
where we kill time, shuteye,
waiting for your key to turn.

Fourth Floor

I reason with the crown of the tree.
Surely from this fourth floor window,
we are equals now. I calculate
the trajectory, would it catch me
if I threw myself into its arms?

I comb for clues from the uneasy rocking
of the branches, the slow swim
of its fingers stirring the air.
There must be something in the moth

flutterings of the mylar balloon;
a pincered ghost trapped
between the twigs,
despite the wind being its ally.

You can't blame the Poplar
for wanting to hoard it.
The only fruit it has ever held onto,
and is now capable of bearing.

Jocale (Five for Silver)

The word 'jewel' was anglicized from the Old French "jouel"
and beyond that, to the Latin word "jocale", meaning plaything.

Never one for the magpie's eye,
avid as the pawnbroker's magnifier,
the mesmerized quarry of the tinsel shine.

Never the gilded valentine, the decorated
lover on parade, the brandisher of a cariad's
rapture with a trifling bauble.

Never the squirreller of trinkets,
the hoarder, the purser, the trover,
the chary archivist of the rhinestone nest.

Never one to grasp the whimsy of dearness,
the pretty penny dwarfed, the wild tender
vaulted in a precious metal's brevity.

Never once starry-eyed by the dangling carat,
still I accepted your ex-fiancee's diamond.
At that ungainly moment in the autumn

New York woods, I wish I had resigned
myself to your secondhand proposal
with the regalia of a *Coke* ring.

White Gold (Six for Gold)

*Married magpies do not steal trinkets and are manifestly scared
of shiny objects. It is supposed that bachelor magpies steal shiny
objects in an attempt to woo potential mates.*

The proposal was a diamond in a dime bag –
a precious stone weeded out
from its previous engagement.

Uprooted, unanchored, the crystal
cornered itself in the plastic purse
like a swan-song line of cocaine.

To the magpie's eye, you were a dealer
on bended knee, pleading me to concede,
to cave into the meagre dope for tender.

*All morning, I had been rehearsing
a way to finally
put an end to us.*

I asked for a ring of Welsh Gold,
settled for the cheapest White Gold,
mostly nickel, from the Jeweller on the Bridge.

*What did it matter, after all,
when its very kernel was salvage,
something old, something borrowed?*

You handed me the obvious box on Christmas Day.
I inched off the paper, unclamped the jaws
to reveal a scrolled piece of paper,

wordless ticker-tape, nothing else –
a sundered cracker with only
the blank joke as its bounty.

Junk Metal

The ring was ferreted out
amongst a gift of men's socks,
a crooked joke incurably lost.

The band slid down the bone
into the valley of the laziest fingers.
My thumb took to twisting the metal,

a fidgety tic that kept
the white gold spinning
in perpetual orbit.

That was until the black rash flared.
A shadow that tattooed the skin,
scorching the ring finger,

the baby finger, the middle finger,
the brink of the palm. It was the acid
of my skin eating away the junk metal.

Could my vitriol corrode
this ring entirely? Leaving
just a diamond in a dime bag,

set aside for cutting
the leaden air of this house,
the glass of your humours.

The Virtual Family
(Eight for a Wish)

*During the breeding season, the magpie hen can
often be identified by having bent or damaged tail feathers.*

Now that I have all I think
I ever wanted; a clutch of cells
coalescing into someone else,
a man who wishes to marry me,
whose voice is a continent away.

With this family-in-waiting,
I shuffle between the wasted rooms
in this wonting spinster nest;
where I have mislaid the thrill
of the loneliness I made here.

I am battening against another single
glazed winter. The curtains ripple
like pole dancers in the window.
A garrison of door snakes
fail to outwit the draughts.

I take long baths to keep warm, delete
time, watch the tap tick, summon the verve
to wash myself. I gaze at the mould
pricking the ceiling, swearing
witness to the slightest cartoon.

Everything shivers with this slow present,
where I am boiled down to a shipwreck
on a couch, bandaged in a sheepskin throw.
The hot water bottle pressed to my gut, I let
the television do the talking for me.

I would hibernate this whole stretch
away if I could, so long as you remember
to wake me when the visceral family
has arrived. When they are more
than a phone call, more than an ache.

Something Else
(Ten for a Bird That's Best To Miss)

*Magpie nests are usually domed to prevent predation
and nest robberies by other crows, namely carrion crows.*

A meanness has become me
since that piss wand harbinger,
blue-lined us the nuclear
family.

And the sickness
is something else,
something else
entirely.

Whatever is swelling
in this brackish gut,
does not
belong;

the crazing of the cuckoo
egg in the dome
of the magpie's
nest.

The curdling of my morning
took me traipsing miles today
to the stepping stones
and back.

The house is freezing, even
with the heating on full.
I have cellophaned
the windows.

The hot water bottle has become
my husband. I clutch it
to my stomach like
a lifebuoy.

I heave with each stair,
relieved at the landing.
I have lost the gumption
to read in bed.

I am wide
awake in the thick
of a puddle, figuring
the water bottle has leaked.

And the pain
is something else,
something else entirely.
Unable to contain itself,

it is flooding
out of me. I stagger
to the bathroom, stutter
a prayer to keep the last of him in.

Pyjamas rusted,
white thighs spoiled,
tannin-stained china,
the silt of near life.

Cold flannel between me,
I make myself decent again,
recoil to your side of bed,
the blank half, unable to change the sheets.

Is it too late
to call anyone or too early?
I can never tell. Too dark for bird
song and the water bottle is still warm.

This Was the Spring

This was the season the lambs were born frozen.
When the hill farmer burrowed through snow
for the opaque flock, cocooned in the camouflage

of immeasurable white. Even then he had to choose
who was to be cloaked over his shoulders and trudged
to asylum or left to shiver in derelict wonder.

Older sheep can brave a life of ice for weeks,
watered by the snow melting around them, feeding
on the wool of their kith, the warmth of their kind.

Still many survivors will die soon after,
not to be buried beneath their native fields,
the petrified grasses they never ventured beyond.

Instead the perished flock becomes a flung mound,
a dune of pillows primed for collection,
pallid, unbloodied, a snowdrift stained.

Net Curtain

The net curtain might have the answer.
After all, she is a perforated eyelid,
a bridal veil between sundered worlds.

The breeze draws her out, sucks
her through the open sash window,
the bubble gum balloon after the burst.

The spring wind expels her back
into the room with a laboured sigh,
a smoker's exhalation between grateful lugs.

He is toying with her now, flirting with her
madly. He sweeps her again off her feet.
Her indecision becomes clockwork.

Argos Wedding

1.

The wedding queue at Worth
Street City Hall, Manhattan

is akin to the wait
at Alton Towers.

We are given a butcher's ticket,
the usherette has a handgun.

We keep watching the screen
for our number to come up.

I tell my sister-in-law in waiting,
this is just like Argos.

Who knew you could buy a wedding
bouquet from a vending machine?

Our witnesses are your Bronx ice hockey team,
your Minnesotan sister.

I am the only thing here
that belongs to me.

2.

I clap shut my compact, shatter
the mirror inside. I laugh

at the seven-year hex I've divined,
minutes before our half-hearted vows.

The armed usherette orders the witnesses
to get out of line. Most of the marrying

are dressed in sweat pants. Still they glare
at me, cradling my splintered mirror,

as if I have cursed this conveyor belt
of non-committal brides.

The Birds of Rhiannon

Before I was mortal, I was haloed
in feathers, my trinity of familiars;
whose birdsong was legend, serenading
the dead from their dreams, lullabying
the living to torpor. For the sake
of this world and him, I swallowed
my companions, let them nest in my belly
and take turns in my throat. The sparrow
became my repartee, my grappling chatter
that flutters away the dead air. The mockingbird
staked claim as my mimicking tongue, parodying
the world as it heard it, to be droll,
to belong. And the thrush was poetry,
my childsong, my verse-voice, the brittle
thread to my blueprint life.

For the sake of my world and him,
I crowded my belly with children.
Each deafened in utero by the never-ending
twittering. My birds heckled my sons
for mirroring the man that caged
them within this ungenerous flesh.
My unborn tried walling their ears,
even taking their leave before
they were finished. My pets pecked
and fought over what remained.
But now that a girl is unfurling,
the facsimile of me, their familiar,
they coo and brood over her, sing her
to flower, while laying eggs of their own
under her unspeakable tongue.

Blodeuwedd

When I took the powers of the oak and the broom
and the meadowsweet, and made them woman,
that was a great wrong —to give those powers a
thinking mind. — The Owl Service

I am now a nighty rover
Banished to the ivy tree — anon

I am Flower Face,
conjured not born.
I am alchemised from earth,
not the humdrum of bone.

My DNA is flora. I am chimera,
a mosaic of petals, a Molotov
cocktail of meadowsweet,
broom, oak blossom.
I bleed syrup and sap.

My meadowsweet, mead wort,
bride wort, grows in dampness.
I am the strewing herb
to scent your floors, I almond
your stewed fruit. I am tea
for your gout and fever,
aspirin for your acid gut.

I am the gorse flowers of broom,
I thrive in parched ground.
I am dyers broom, jaundicing your wool.
I am salad, raw, pickled,
I poison your pregnancy.
I am the hanging catkin of oak,
a ticking time bomb of pollen.

2.

I am the primeval catalogue bride,
Gwydion and Math's balmy invention;
a cure for the cursed
Lleu Llaw Gyffes, blighted
by his own abandoning mother
to never be loved by a human woman.

I am the pig-brained wedding gift,
embroidering an invented life,
this manufactured marriage.
I thread petals into stitches,
caging them within the warp
and weft of this wifery.

When this husband moves inside me,
I pestle and mortar myself, decant
the pot pourri of me into the fissures
of this marital chamber.

I draught myself back to the cloaking
crinoline of the Oak, the soft
scurry of birds and insects inside me.
I replant myself in the meadow,
sink back into the cwtch
of the docile soil.

I would uproot the stones of this prison
if I could, reclaim my shelter
under the roof of the fickle,
Welsh sky, as it hoofs down
its ocean upon me.

3.

I am now the white mask, squashed,
heartface of a barn owl.
I am elderberry eyes,
fingers arthritic with talons.

I am the tattered cloak of wheat,
the moth's wing beat. I am hunter,
butcher, enemy of birds, tethered
to the night like a haunting.

I am witchbird, ju–ju, amulet for evil,
I am caterwaul, screech owl,
banshee scream, piccolo hoot,
a cry of mourning.

I am the retort of *Too Whit*
to my dead lover's silence.
And what are feathers anyway?
But unbreakable flowers.

PART TWO

It Is

the revelation of the runny yolk
after the egg has been scalped;

the hand-written letter on the doormat
like the glimpse of a rare bird;

the sip that attests to the alchemy
of perfectly sweetened tea;

the clemency of dressing yourself
in clothes hung and warmed by the fire;

the fluent descent of the coffee plunger;
the smell of toast, the unrivalled char of it;

the unearthing of a mix tape from your first love;
the relief of a decent barrister against your ex;

the thrill of the toilet effervescing
in a flood of royal blues;

the twelve-week scan that testifies
to proof of life.

Poems in the Dock

Her poems have been subpoenaed, summonsed
by the ex-husband to give witness testimony
against the mental health of their author.

All morning they have been scrolling through
their funeral/interview fonts, disrobing the habitual
Courier, settling for a more sincere *Calibri*.

The poems request a separate waiting room
to their accuser, who is representing himself again.
They wring their hands, second-guessing their line breaks.

Parents' Evening is called to the stand. Her twin
verses trembling. She is cross-examined
on the intent behind her matricidal last line.

She loses her nerve, confesses she was a one
draft wonder composed under the influence
in her ex-boyfriend's parlour.

The district judge prompts her to remember herself.
She recalls she is a childhood list poem, mother dying
was a fear not a wish. She is swiftly dismissed.

Gravy, *Suitcase* and *Marital Visit* are called as a cluster,
to substantiate the poet's diminished moral character.
They claim the Sally Bowles Defence, defer to juvenilia.

Girl Meats Boy is called, the jukebox staple,
the bookend to a decade of set readings.
Her rhymes sit smugly in their John Tripp tiara.

The redundant husband accuses the poem of cannibalism,
misandry; which dictated the tone of the marriage,
corroborating the unhinged mind behind her.

The poem counsels the plaintive. She was composed
six years before he ever read her. If he was honest
with himself, he never truly got her.

This Is The Drawer

where orphan buttons are born,
where the relics of our cotton marriage
are interred. Here is the clip-on
bow tie from our wedding day,
the compact mirror I shattered
in the queue to our vows.

Here is the thistle glass jewel box,
the bone yard for the rite-of-passage pearls,
the crossless Dali crucifix,
the beads made by your mother,
the Mexican choker from the poet,
I never found an occasion to wear.

Here is the sapphire from SP's Mother,
who still remembers my birthday,
the amethyst engagement ring
from my eighteen-year-old love,
the crystal bib necklace
from my dead friend's wedding.

A pair of *Audrey Hepburn* gloves,
a key for our daughter's window,
Nana's Eisteddfod medal for singing,
your wedding ring left for scrap,
my 50 and 100 metre swimming badges
never sewn to my costume.

"Describe The Pain"

The doctor staples her thumb into my extremities:
Wrists, knuckles, phalanges, toes and soles.
Is this my cue to wince, flinch with histrionics,
kick like a bygone frog brimming with electric charge?

I am failing her as the patient and the incidental poet,
as I ransack the gurney for the pitch
perfect adjective, just as a rifle for a poem
that deserves to be borstaled.

Your sliding scale of one to ten
is only an abacus of stamina;
the fortitude to shrug away
or feebly endure.

Are *dull, stabbing* and *throbbing* the only
pains on the menu? What if the ache has taken
root? The sly guest with squatter's rights,
a livid twin absorbed.

The Abacus of Stamina

There is the me who diarises her day
by rationing the stair climbs;
who strews pillows like mock stepping
stones to the sirening of the cot.

There is the me who hangs her hands
under the scalding water tap;
to recapture the fingers frozen
perpendicular in the night.

There is the me whose wrist vein bulges,
whose knuckles have swollen vague,
who cannot hoist a mug to her lips,
uses the pushchair as a Zimmer frame.

Where is the me who was a sprinter,
a district tennis champion, a climber
who could scale the Mile End wall and slink
up the rope in gym like a coconut cutter?

There is the me who flounders with buttons,
who cannot shell a tampon of its plastic,
is unable to dangle her daughter by the ankles,
barely leaves an impression with her pen.

The Art of Fastening

These fingers are chopsticks, decrypting
the riddle of buttoning your school blouse.
My fumbles fall down the ladder of your shirt,
trying to remaster the trick of twisting,
flipping four-eyed moons through a hole.

My three-year-old tenders a helping hand,
a starfish, ham-fisted, yanking
at discs and thread. This only kindles
the dread of these gutless fingers making
stabs at sewing the buttons back on.

Who knew the coiling of bobbles
around plaits could capsize me?
The cat cradling between index and thumb
could collapse under an elastic band's tension;
now that hair must be tied to ward off lice.

Before your wardrobe was painless,
your hair given free rein. It now takes
a dexterity; a smiling sticker
you have yet to earn, while my art
of fastening fritters away.

Dear Rain

You are my nemesis, dear Rain;
singing to the iron in my blood,
brittling it to rust by morning.

Do you percolate the bedroom air by osmosis?
Drench my dreaming inhalations
to unscrew the hinges of my bones.

This golf umbrella is kowtowing to you.
It has surrendered its shield, blunting
my signature marches to callipered steps.

My homeland has its lion's share of you,
you are the only resource left for the taking.
Your waters drain me, dear Rain.
Here where the heavens are forever ajar.

Threnody

i.m. Enid Hughes (1928 to 2015)

Teach me to wear a kaftan, Enid:
To have a dining room table
entirely devoted to *Scrabble*.
Teach me to fill in the *Daily Mail* crossword
with what *I think* are the right answers.

Teach me to have a garage, a catacomb for wine,
fireworks of flowers bursting from the garden.
Teach me to have a beaded curtain
instead of a kitchen door; to populate
my hallway with graduating grins,
which my Stannah Stairlift inches past.

Teach me to travel the world in a Murvi,
the zipping slide of the closing van's door.
Teach me to build a wall of tupperware boxes
to seal a life time's work of Welsh cakes.
Teach me to bugger off to Malaga
for my arthritis and learn Sevillanna
instead of the language.

Teach me to perfume my kitchen with garlic
and vinegar, to fill my tea caddies with sugar
sachets stolen from service stations.
Teach me to tauten the air with arguments
and your daughters will argue back,
because they are your daughters.

Teach me your feather laugh,
that tinkles like toasting crystal.
Teach me the slow swish of your wrist,
the unhurried smile that makes
the room smile with you.

Teach me to shout '*David*' like a whip-crack,
making your husband snap to attention.
Teach him to say '*Yesi Mawr!*'
in strained exclamation
from wherever he may be hiding.

Teach me to stroll the corridors
of Ysgol Castell Newydd, glasses dangling
at my breasts and more keys than sense
bouncing on my hip. Teach the Dalmatian
Lady to trot by my side.

Teach me to dance with your sister Mavis,
who spent her infancy in leg braces.
Teach me her gap-toothed chuckle.

Teach me to see your father Danny Buster,
who taught you to make money in the snooker hall.
Teach me about your mother Edith,
who had a ration book for laughter.

Teach me about a husband you have known
since you were eight years old.
Teach me to roll down Caerphilly mountain,
abandoning your clothes and what the world
thought at the mynydd's peak.

Teach me about David's glorious smile,
the whitening ginger of his beard,
the inverted commas
of his dimples.

Teach me to wear a silk kaftan, Enid Hughes:
to sit throned at the Scrabble table,
with a long glass of *Rosé*
beside the nonsensical letters.

And even though David is losing his mind
and you are arbitrarily keeping score,
he was always destined to beat you
in this unwinnable game.

David

i.m. David Hughes (1926 to 2016)

What will I miss? I'll tell you what I'll miss. Colours starting
(Nothing in Particular – Hugo Williams)

I will miss his folded arms,
hands tucked inside the vice
of his *Slazenger* pullover armpits.

I will miss his crossed ankles,
the squeaking of leather
as he rubbed his shoes together.

I will miss him seesawing with laughter,
a human rocking chair, straitjacketing
his mirth in the wrapping of his limbs.

I will miss his V-necked golf sweaters,
him leaning in towards me, forefinger frozen
like a child's gun, to punctuate his argument.

I will miss his Baptist minister enunciation
of each individual syllable in words
like *lavatory* and *homosexual.*

I will miss the clacking of car keys in his hand,
the walnut dash of the Red Maxi,
the sunburnt smell of its leather seats.

I will miss him in the driving seat
of the blue Murvi, feeding the steering wheel
through his hands like a bus driver,

I will miss his waiting 'la dee dee dah' number,
for which no lyrics have ever been written
and no real melody composed.

I will miss the arcs scoring his cheek
as he grinned, the ripples in a pond
after the pebble has struck.

I will miss the revelation of that rare smile,
teeth filling his face with a fervour
like lifting the lid on a piano.

Kay

She sits before the boiler,
guarding its pulse,
warming her back.

Her props are a mug of *Nescafé*, milk,
two sugars, *Berkeley Blue* in the ashtray,
Elkie Brooks on the cassette player.

She is *L'Oréal* blonde to the shoulder,
flicked fringe, *Anais Anais*
on her neck and wrists.

Her Chesterfield market, baggy white jumper
is constant. She pushes the cuffs to her elbows
but the sleeves billow back to her hands.

Jeans flatter her dancers' legs.
She passed the audition to get into Laban
but chose to marry instead.

She accosts the kitchen mirror,
clicks her fingers and swoons,
while the hot brush slowly warms.

Gareth

His eyelid has fallen.
A blood crescent moon
capsized on its side,
cradles a yellowing eye.
It weeps of its own accord.
It would not cry otherwise.

His sunburnt scalp,
red as outback dust,
glares through the whiteness
of still thick hair.

The broken capillaries
of his cheeks are the whipping
scars of a golfing wind.
'Dissipation', his second wife
calls it. 'dypsomania',
says his first.

Fragments of his dinner
swim like plankton
in his glass of Malbec.
With the dip of a napkin,
he shores the debris
and wipes over the brim.

Mother says his almond eyes
have turned piggy with time.
The cornflower blue
has become diluted,
like the bleached basin
of a disused swimming pool.

He hawks and gobs through
the open car window.
The wind reciprocates the gift,
splattering his face
with a bridal veil
of his own embroidery.

Free, No Obligation Valuation

Mr Edwards calls her Judith Chalmers,
as she's always on bloody holiday.
She's a teddy bear smile at your front door,
a valuation pack and business card on your coffee table.

She knows the life story behind every house
on our shelves. She'll make you a cup of tea
in your own kitchen, if you need her to,
she'll always find the right cupboard.

It's just bricks and mortar, she'll assure you,
as you weep at your four walls.
The photos of weddings, births and holidays
that weren't enough to keep the home cemented.

She will describe your house as *'attractive'*
and *'immaculate'* on the dictaphone,
as you dodge the sniper light of the laser
measure darting across your rooms.

She tears her hair out at the computer,
as she gets her comparables together.
You will always get a personal thank you letter,
the following day, first class post.

She can't get through a lager and lime at the *'Spoons*
without an old school friend, asking for a val.
Sometimes, Rhi', I've just got to go with my gut.
You ever tried cooking chicken in Coke?

Make Clos Pwll Clai Property of the Week, will you?
Tell Craig I'll call him back. Is the mortgage offer out?
Have they commissioned searches on Hazeledene Avenue?
Don't talk to me about Japanese Knotweed.

Adam

In the beginning there was Trevor,
humming of Labradors, pipe tobacco
and *Land Rovers*. His small Yorkshire mouth
spoke in mumbles and boasts, often lost
in his beard before they reached your ear.

And Trevor wedded Jean, the scholarship girl,
who kept working class friends,
a cigarette holder for her *Café Cremes*,
playing *Patience* on the floor
with two decks of cards.

And they begat Adam, swinging with moods,
tantrums that bought him solitary
under the stairs. As a child,
he would tape-record breakfast,
sleep with the radio to his ear,

laugh when you hurt him.
Out of his hysterics came silence.
As a man, he behaves in the company
of boats, though forever parched,
spitting feathers on dry land.

He races through a 24-pack of *Carling*,
reels in the road on his untrusty sea legs.
He blights conversation with dope fables,
the injustice of why he keeps getting fired,
tiring anyone who listens or loves him.

He turns ancient in a matter of hours,
sucking his thumb by the end of the night.

I still see the toddler, luminous with pride.
The day he staggered up to his father,
presented him with a potty brimming
with piss, as if bequeathing him
the gold of a wise man's gift.

I Remember Being You,

pigeon-toed pretty, long-haired
on a train. I remember having
time to slowly tuck away
the strays, before bobbles
became my bracelet, ponytails
became my trademark.

I remember having room
for that new paperback novel.
The one gazing up at you,
in no hurry to be read,
the bisecting bookmark,
the unbroken spine.

I remember the neatness
of being you, life mapped
out on a flip tray: The purse
without a stretch-mark,
the uncracked face
of the mobile phone.

Regard your erudite choice
of coffee, bought with ample
time to spare. The plastic
lid visibly kissed
with the lightness
of the Pope's ring.

I Am Turning

into the woman who affixes
the stickers of her house number
to the face of her recycling bins.

I am mirroring the kinks of my spotless mother,
tweezing the trespassing fluff between my fingers,
as it tumbleweeds the carpet of the stairs.

I am edifying into a judicious pot washer,
who dries and returns pans and dishes
in the ordered strata of the drawers.

I am in raptures over the new pedal bin.
How it sits perfectly in the sliver
between the backdoor and the drier.

I am sophisticating into a paragon of symmetry,
aligning the furniture with the planked edges
of the engineered oak flooring I bought on sale.

I am revising the presentation
of the bath towels in the tall boy,
that are now scrolled instead of folded.

I am no longer the accidental ghost,
who, for twenty years, potholed blindly
inside the cavern of her duvet cover.

I am now the mistress of the house,
having mastered the bloated sail of the duvet
and learned to marry the unruly corners.

★★★★★

I am the seasoned maid, who rings
a brass bell in the hallway to chime
the readiness of her daughter's meals.

I am the conscientious dietician, who ensures
three fruits in her daughter's breakfast,
four vegetables smuggled into dinner.

I am the culinary artist, who prohibits
two foods of the same colour
to be touching on her daughter's plate.

I am the faithful archivist, who compiles
portfolios of every picture and painting,
her daughter has ever drawn.

I am the diligent curator, who prints,
dates and names every person in every photo
of her daughter's life, even naming myself.

Identity Theft

It started as an idle joke:
Your friend Adriana ran away
with my birthday photograph.
She made a cut-out of your ex's face,
superimposed it upon my own.

Look at this doctored family portrait:
My predecessor's unfamiliar features
holding court at my fortieth,
clutching my daughter's hand,
my age badged upon her breast.

I have taken the joke too far, you say,
as I paste this newly unearthed face
onto every milestone, every album,
like newspaper letters
glued to a kidnapping note.

I now see her microbladed brows,
well-rested eyes, looking up to camera,
cradling my newborn. Her ebony-tonged
curls pour out of the mortar
at my university graduation.

I peruse her botoxed forehead,
line-betraying grin, photoshopped
onto my wedding picture.
This revised bride is positively
beaming, without a shadow of doubt.

Is this not the same thirty-something
swaddled in my mother's arms?
Who cannot love that come-hither smile,
as she is returned to the incubator,
without a shred of jaundice on her.

The Trees Have Dimmed

The trees have dimmed their bark
to usher in this night. Soft fog
squats over the frozen field;
a flying carpet, an astral projection
of ground suspended in self-regard.

The mist slices the calves of the last
standing men, martyrs to the elements,
religious dog-walkers, unwitting
to the winter trickery of clouds
gathering about them.

One man marches on the spot, breathing
into the den of his ungloved hands.
White smoke balloons from his fagless mouth;
an extinguished dragon, the embers
of a fire-eater's supper.

Swallows bail with each chilled
exhalation and frigid word.
A sheepdog paws at the dirt, kicks
up particles of white dust. He summons
a brume, exhumes the ghost of himself.

Return of the Native

The wooden bench is sinking, reclining
back to nature, reassuming root
in the cradling earth. Long grasses
have ambushed the concrete feet,
jaded mosses upholster the wolfing rot.

The latitude of the grain, the benchmark
of time when it thrived, is fading now.
Arrowed nettles loom through the parallel
cracks, their splayed, praying hands
cushioning the horizontal plain.

Even as a fraction of its elemental self,
it is defying the guise, the grand design,
callous return to earth. It shrinks
to its knees in the quickening soil,
swallowed by the shade of what it once was.

Soon the camouflage of this pew will be
absolute. And the skeletal fingers
of cow parsley, that have locked their grip
to its backbone, will drag it back
to the grave where the ascendancy began.

Prodigal Audience

i.m. The Embassy Cinema, Bridgend (1939 to 2010)

1

From the derelict bleachers
of a jilted cinema,
where the flip-seats are petrified
in stubborn prayer; a terracotta army,
poised as a domino trail
on tenterhooks
before the flick.

The Embassy flashes back,
back to Pearl and Dean,
back to the MGM lion
roaring in cartouche,
back to a montage where the rope
still tunnelled through the curtains' mind,

before it was dragged out of hiding
like a fugitive python
and the lumbering drapes
slumped to the stage
like fainting dames.

2

This picture house has only ever known
the half-light, a perennial dusk.

This casino blindness slackens
your canny grip upon the hour.

A hailstorm of popcorn,
bullets through projection dust,

where the most innocent coupling
can mutate in the dark.

3

In this palace of pigeons,
it is packed to the rafters,
feathers spluttering and drifting
like crisps wafting back to earth.

You can only speculate
the film was a resounding hit
by the flying ovation,
the cooing of encores
from popcorn-sized lungs.

4

This screen wall that only ever caught
the shadow puppetry of the motion picture,
the residue of the projection's lustre,
is being clawed from its corners,

hacked from its sides
by a wheeze of clumsy robotics,
a long-necked dinosaur footed
in a war tank's rubber crawlers.

This clatter of sci-fi Jurassic
tears brick, the ribs of girders.
Arrows of light perforate the belly
of the theatre that has gone dark for good.

It triggers the muscle memory of a pulley,
wheeling the phantom pleats apart on cue
to the flickering of life
cartooning in its folds.

5

The Embassy blinks like a mole,
wincing at the alabaster day,
the overcast canvas, unwitnessed
since the walls closed in.

The sky is quick to bag the role
of the once woven screen,
the virgin skin to the twitching
tattoo of Pen-y-Bont ar Ogwr,
a foolhardy town unreeling itself.

This cult classic is in low resolution,
tarnished technicolor and specless 3-D,
with a surround sound that makes you brackish
with the tremor of bulldozers,
the hectoring of a pneumatic drill
cross-examining your bones.

6

The plot churns like cement
in the drum, as an epic cast
is unearthed, the Embassy's own
prodigal audience.

We circle the felled wall,
the spine of the screen,
catch our first sight of the Gods,
the invasive white orchid

climbing the walls,
the balcony, the front row,
half a century of impressions,
cushion dents, the hollows
of forgotten thrones.

7

I have become the voyeur
from the wrong side,
the lily-livered spectator
to this final public screening.

I hang on every craven word,
rapt, on the edge, the suspense
killing, alone as a tourist
forgotten on the film set.

PART THREE

Thinner

Now we have come together at featherweight.
You all unpinchable gangle, me with this
eroded jawline and glockenspiel décolletage.

We weren't always this way, I've seen
the pudding proof, the captured convex
of our bellies, pouched faces without angles.

You chased away your stones, marathon
miles at a time, pedalled them up mountains,
dissolved them in breast strokes.

I panicked off my pounds, spry
under house arrest, my fat absconded
under the audit of a perishing husband.

All I saw was your thinness at first,
eyes turned kind with tiredness,
a head I could platter in my palm.

I discarded you as too slight
for loving. Even whittled down,
I would crush you.

We fill the bed with our foreign bodies,
our stomachs groaning, see-sawing
on the pebbles of each other's hipbones.

He Is The Kind

of man who clicks his fingers at the radio,
discards teabags on the draining board,
despite my navigations to the compost bin.

He is the kind of man who wears nothing
in the morning except an unruly cardigan, quotes
Winnicott while stirring honey into his porridge.

He is the kind of man who makes a beeline
for my bookcase, wears his silent
reading like an invisibility cloak.

He is the kind of man who calls me 'baby',
divining my mother's caveat that only
the unfaithful bless you with a pet name.

He is the kind of man who is languid
in his crumbling Audi, sheds his seatbelt
like my bra strap, when compelled to reverse.

He is the kind of man who brings
two mugs of tea to bed in the morning,
both of which are for himself.

He is the kind of man who eats only half
a banana, bandaging the needless remainder
in the blackening of its skin.

My Clocks Pester Him

He gagged the alarm clock, buried
her alive in the knicker drawer;
unhung the faux French wall clock,
smothered her ticks in the dirty laundry.

He made himself at home
by dislodging their batteries;
froze their panicked hands mid-air,
rendering them dumb. Heartless.

What of the novelty bird clock
with twelve species of tweet?
How did she meet her untimely demise
to never again chirp on the hour?

Did he have to dig out the tongue
of the innocuous carriage clock?
The letter opener lying by her side
like a murder weapon. She never sung again.

How I miss my metronomic circus;
the unsynchronised pulse of my rooms;
my ornamental pets Morse-coding one
another across the gulf of the hallway.

In this loveless silence, this paralysis
of time, I tap my impatient sole,
tock my bitten tongue, percussing
the hourglass of our untouching hands.

In A Relationship (Pending)

Now I have said it, I pedal
frantically towards a future.
Although the survey declares (us)
structurally unsound,
in need of underpinning.

Now I have said it, I extend
the house to make room (for you).
I have stock-piled the cupboards
with Gluten, Lactose Free. I have even
allen-keyed (together) a desk in my bedroom
to aid your escape from my noise.

Will I get used to your flung shoes
tripping over one another? Your books
bogarting every surface, your clothing
in molehills, nothing (ever)
returned to the fridge?

Now I have announced us to my World
(web jury). Despite the 42 'likes',
you keep us dangling in Siberia:
'in a relationship (pending)',
withholding your single click of accord.

Circling

I have been circling this comatose phone
like a vulture withdrawing from crack.
It has been 37.5 hours since your last communication.
Your mobile must be lost, stolen even.

Perhaps you caught them mid-burglary?
Did they duct-tape and gag you,
bundle you in the wardrobe
where you are now struggling for air?

Was it during your shift on the cuckoo ward?
Did your favourite patient stab you
with your own prescription specs, taking
the time to amputate your scribing fingers?

Did your Airbnb guest bludgeon you
in your sleep? Or worse, seduce you?
Did you do it for the online review,
to maintain your five star rating?

Perhaps your poetry group turned postal,
curdled by your feedback. Did they take
it in turns to crucify you, leaving a stigmata
of blue blood from their fountain pen nibs?

Maybe you went for a solitary run,
twisted your Achilles again? A kindly
farmer must have found you and shot you
in the skull to put you out of my misery.

Dare I send you a kissless SOS?
Mail you an unblinking carrier pigeon,
recorded delivery? Or hurl my heart
in a bottle in 140 characters or less?

Slapstick

Look at this daft nudity:
infants caught in the act,
our curiosity collapsed.

Now that our bodies have ridiculed
the open water of our skin,
peeled in all its pale ruin.

We claw for the scraps,
dress with slapstick celerity
against the clumsy disrobing.

Our costumes bury the chagrin,
bandage and armour,
rewind and rewrite us
out of this blundering passion.

I Took The First Lust

I took the first lust as gospel,
our oblivion to one another,
the fluke of our collision.

I took our rapture for granted,
convinced it would tend to us,
shepherd and abet us.

We were marooned on your bed.
You made no bones about yourself,
matter-of-factly versed me

in becoming a selfish lover.
Still I tried every trick
in the book, applied myself

with automated rigour, took you
to the brink of torture.

Just give me fruition, finality,
la petite mort, the money shot
that stubbornly refuses to come.

Fatter

Now I am returning to my fighting weight,
a rubber ring of flesh girdling my waist
to save me from drowning, again.

I undress for bed, safe behind the screen
of the wardrobe door. I re-robe to the brim,
underwear, pyjamas buttoned to the nape.

You lie naked against the pillows,
proud of your boy body,
the face of a fifty-year-old man.

You idly inquire whether I've put on
a few pounds, continuing to write
in your diary, not looking up.

Now I have fattened to a woman's size 10,
still fitting the clothes you once unzipped.
I ask if you find me less attractive.

You are candid at least, bold in admitting
what no man probably should, preferring
the heroin chic of when we first met.

I deemed you too slight for loving then,
knowing there was too much of me,
even when there was nothing of me.

Love and Taxes

Who knew the arc of us could be charted
through a year's cache of receipts?
Dealt with the precision of a croupier,
a tarot reader. A notable absence

of train tickets during our honeymoon months,
where the offers to drive me home
came with no trouble, a pleasure. The sudden
appearance of return journeys for £31.30.

The countless dinners that weren't Dutch:
Bells in Bristol, Browns in Laugharne,
posh burgers in Winchester,
Sunday lunch at the Windmill.

An itemised receipt of Lactose Free
milk for your morning tea, Soy for your porridge,
Gluten Free bread, pasta, the brownie mix,
I never got around to baking for you.

An Ikea receipt for the desk I bought
to make you stay a while longer. Dunelm's proof
of purchase for soundless clocks, blackout curtains,
your specifications for sleep that never came.

Paper-clipped by month, bulldogged by year,
I coral my expenses by date, by category,
retain only the deductible scraps of you
to renew my claim for credit.

Handover

I keep an eye out for your second-hand,
silver Audi. Cycle rack on the roof,
where our bikes rode for miles
without turning a wheel.

You're surprised I even
agreed to meet. You take
off your trainers, help
yourself to a glass of water.

We sit across from each other.
You shift to my side.
Your hand finds my shoulder.
My hand finds your knee.

After all these months, we still
tumble into the habit
of each other. I swerve
away from your kiss.

I hand over your things:
Kate Bush CD, green shirt,
toothbrush, *Wild Sargasso Sea*,
which I never finished,

your box of Earl Grey.
You return a handful
of books you never
asked to borrow.

You reclaim your mountain bike
out of the woodshed, with the mildewed
seat I had bleached, half an hour earlier.
You strap it to the roof of the car.

We hug. I kiss you on the cheek.
You kiss me on the mouth. I walk
across to my side of the road.
I don't look back.

No Harm In Him

You stand in the shower like a bouncer,
you-ain't-on-the-list smile
creased across your face.
Your glasses remain in their lawful place,
car windscreens in the rain, fogged, soap-streaked,
as the water hoofs down on you.
You shave your scalp closer than *Kojak*.

You were Llanelli's answer to the *Milky Bar Kid*.
A shock of white blonde hair, NHS specs
that could sun-fry a colony of ants.
Your brothers tickled you daft
until you peed your pants, locked
you in the airing cupboard, ran away,
chanting *mammy doesn't love you*.

Your fiancée deflowered you.
She tore your banjo string
while you were still learning love.
Who knew there would be so much blood?
You crushed the nurse's hand
as you were stitched back together.
A convoy of junior doctors came in to observe.

Your first wife was a Jehovah's witness,
migratory, a gypsy soul. Barely months
in a new house, you would come
home to another *For Sale* board. You elected
for a vasectomy at thirty, to discover
a daughter in waiting. The crayoned *Dear John*,
you thought the children had written.

Your second wife cheated with a mutual friend:
The geologist with the scarred jaw,
a poor man's *Action Man*, a wolf in chav clothing.
He used to come over for barbecues with his kids.
Your stepdaughter spilled the beans,
thought you had a right to know. Her mother
tried to get her fake nails on your pension.

Now you're a grandfather, midnight feasting
on *Netflix*, *Haribo* jellies and *Tanqueray* gin,
pointing the wall of your cottage on weekends.
You make raspberry cheesecake and tiramisu
from scratch, share it with the boys
on the factory floor for their honest-
to-God opinion.

Here you are standing in my shower,
feet fanned, freckled arms crossed,
mouth tinged with liquorice vape
that you suck like a Ventolin inhaler.
Morning meetings are the death of you,
you call HR the smiling assassins.
I ask you what a *gunt* and a *wizard's sleeve* is.

I am learning to decipher your codes:
That you complain you're pieing out,
that people are bulbing us because you're punching.
That most of your sentences begin
with a Kung fu masterly *so*.
That *odd-ee-oh* means audio.
That your *want* rhymes with pant.

The Addiction Counsellor

has a tranquilizing voice.
He wears his glasses on his scalp,
the crown of an understated prince.

The addiction counsellor's irises
are tucked far behind his crow's feet.
I edge closer than fiduciary allows
to discern the colours I am dealing with.

I confess to the addiction counsellor
that I'm not really addicted to anything.
He informs me to the contrary, tells me
I am hungry to be touched.

The addiction counsellor has feathers
instead of fingers. He holds my hipbones
lightly as he passes me in the doorway.

I have stopped listening to the addiction
counsellor, my attention rapt
with his futon in the room next door.

The addiction counsellor gifts me a bottle
of Moët for buying my very first house.
The addiction counsellor asks me
if his gesture is too much.

I tell my daughter on the way to nursery,
the addiction counsellor puts butterflies
in Mummy's tummy. She rightly reprimands
me for wolfing butterflies again.

Acknowledgements

Some of the poems have appeared in the *Spectator*, *Poetry Wales*, *Scintilla*, the *Lampeter Review*, *The High Window*, *Poetry at Sangam* and some of these poems previously appeared in the illustrated pamphlet 'Brood' (Seren 2017).

I would like to acknowledge Literature Wales for the Time Off Work bursary to write my second collection, The Carnegie House Artist Residency commission, which became *Prodigal Audience*, the Vernon Watkins Centenary commission from Swansea University, which became *The Art of Fastening*, the podcast commission from Bedtime Stories For The End of The World, which became *Blodeuwedd*. *Slapstick* and *I Took The First Lust As Gospel* formed part of a commission and multi media dance, music, poetry and art production *Soft Touch / Hard Heart* on the subject of erectile dysfunction. Some of these poems were the fruits of my pregnant writers residency and bird obsession at Aberystwyth Arts Centre in 2012.

I would like to thank the invaluable feedback from everyone at *Answers on a Postcard*, Julie Griffiths, Tracey Rhys, Amanda Rackstraw, Susie Wild, Mab Jones, Emily Cotterill, Emily Blewitt and Kali Hughes, the mentorship of Philip Gross, the constancy of Hugo Williams, the eyes and ears of Paul Deaton, the unflagging support of Amy Wack, the patience of the Seren attic, my second family at Gareth L Edwards Ltd and my first and foremost family that is my father and employer Gareth Edwards, my mother Kay Hughes and my raison d'etre Megan Harwell.